T0209355

TWO CREATIONS:

BARA

AND

ASAH

EMMANUEL J CHARLES

WESTBOW
PRESS®
A DIVISION OF THOMAS NELSON
& ZONDERVAN

WestBow Press books may be ordered through booksellers or by contacting:

WestBow Press
A Division of Thomas Nelson & Zondervan
1663 Liberty Drive
Bloomington, IN 47403
www.westbowpress.com
844-714-3454

Unless otherwise indicated, all Scripture are taken from
King James version of the Bible, public domain.

Scriptures marked (ASV) are taken from The Holy Bible,
American Standard Version (ASV), public Domain.

ISBN: 979-8-3850-0663-2 (sc)
ISBN: 979-8-3850-0664-9 (hc)
ISBN: 979-8-3850-0665-6 (e)

Library of Congress Control Number: 2023916858

Print information available on the last page.

WestBow Press rev. date: 09/15/2023

CONTENTS

PREFACE

The creation account, according to Genesis 1, is literal based on logical reasoning, scientific evidence, and theological support from the Bible. I will present the comprehensive earth history in accordance with the Genesis creation account and the scientific evidence found in the earth's strata.

The first three verses of the Bible should be considered as three distinct events that took place in four different eras of the earth's history: Precambrian, Paleozoic, Mesozoic, and Cenozoic. The earth's history is not cyclical; rather, it is linear-based.

The first verse—"In the beginning, God created the heaven, and the earth"—consists of the Precambrian, Paleozoic, and Mesozoic eras.

Heaven is 13.8 billion years old, and the earth is 4.6 billion years, minus 66 million years old.

The second verse—"And the earth was without form, and void; and darkness was upon the face of the deep. And the Spirit of God moved upon the face of the waters"—is the beginning of the Tertiary period of Cenozoic era. The timeline is sixty-six million years.

The third verse—"And God said, 'Let there be light'"—is the beginning of re-creation, seven thousand years ago.

The evidence for creation has far greater truths than the theory of evolution because God existed before Genesis 1:1, and in the beginning, he created the heaven and the earth.

The inability to explain creation has become detrimental to the churches and for people of faith. For this reason, many churches have stopped using the Old Testament.

Young students have walked away from faith due to a lack of evidence in refuting the theory of evolution, causing them to have doubts in their Creator. These students were raised in Christian homes in faith.

It has become a monumental task to articulate the creation account in the midst of the lies and deception spilled in our public schools, which teach the big bang theory and evolution as scientific truths.

We can trust and believe the creation account from the book of Genesis because the Word of God is absolute, infallible, and inerrant. God is the Creator of the physical universe and the earth.

Two Creations: Bara and Asah explains the biblical account of theistic creation, according to the book of Genesis 1. It should not be confused with the other creation accounts, such as natural evolution, theistic evolution, day/age creation theory, gap theory, or young or old earth theory. *Two Creations: Bara and Asah* brings out the real earth history that took place, based on creation in Genesis.

The creation account, according to Genesis 1:1–3, is important as it pertains to our understanding of biblical creation.

ONE

FIRST CREATION

In the beginning, God created the heaven and the earth.
—Genesis 1:1

This was the first creation. Scientifically, the universe is estimated to be 13.8 billion years old and the earth is 4.6 billion years old. When the Bible says *heaven*, that includes galaxies beyond galaxies, outer space, our solar system, and the waste sky with atmosphere. After the sun and stars were fully formed, the earth and other planets in our solar system were formed. The earth rotated on its axis and moved in its orbit around the sun, like other planets in our solar system.

Our universe was created by God, according to Genesis 1:1. Heaven is known as the sky, where the birds fly and clouds form. The sun, moon, planets, and stars are situated just above that, including galaxies beyond galaxies. Heaven is 13.8 billion years old. Earth is 4.6 billion years old, according to scientific evidence.

> *bara*, or created: to bring into existence, something out of nothing

Time, energy, space, and matter came into existence at the same time. The Hebrew word for created is *bara*. This word is used in the Bible only for the action of God. No action by humans can be referred to as bara.

> *asah*, or make: to work with the existing materials or things

Bara and *asah* are both Hebrew words mentioned in the creation account with other words, like *yatsar*, which means form, and *banah*, which means build.

It took almost four billion years for the earth to form; this was the Precambrian era. The rocks that were formed during the Precambrian era were considered azoic, meaning having no life. In 1954, however, when upper rocks were examined under a microscope, scientists found single-celled organisms, like bacteria and stromatolites, existed in these rocks.

During the Cambrian period of the Paleozoic era, approximately 550 million years ago, complex creatures suddenly appeared. This is called the Cambrian explosion. God created complex creatures like trilobites and other sea creatures. These Cambrian marine invertebrates appeared suddenly, without any precursor in the preceding strata.

The animal kingdom is divided into thirty-six phyla, and twenty of thirty-six phyla appeared in the Cambrian explosion. Later, during the Paleozoic era, fish, terrestrial plants (such as ferns), first amphibians, sharks, and reptiles were created. Apart from marine creatures, minerals, such as iron and lead, formed during other periods of the Paleozoic era.

Black shale, from which oil, gas, and other fossil fuels are produced, was found in abundance during the Devonian period of the Paleozoic era and the Cretaceous period of the Mesozoic era.

Coal was produced abundantly during the Pennsylvanian period of the Paleozoic era. The coal was formed due to continent-sized floating forests; when they were destroyed by natural catastrophe, such as earthquakes and floods, the hollow trees—made up of only bark— sank to the shallow seabed. The mud which was mixed with water settles slowly forming a half to one-inch-thick clay layer on top of the bark creating a flat surface called benches.

Twelve feet of accumulated bark produced one foot of peat, and six feet of peat produced one foot of coal. These coal beds are found throughout the world, especially in the eastern parts of the United States, Europe, and the western part of Russia.

The biblical geologic time scale is based on the creation account from Genesis 1:1–3.

Biblical Geological Time Scale, 4.6 Billion Years				
Cenozoic		Gen. 1:3	Re-creation	Grass, sea creatures, birds, animals, and humans	7,000 years
	Quaternary	Gen. 1:2 The earth was without form, and void, and darkness was ...		Empty and unfit for life	2 million years
				Water covered the earth	
	Tertiary			It was dark on the surface	64 million years
				Spirit of God was hovering over the waters	

Mesozoic	Cretaceous	First creation: "In the beginning God created heavens and the earth" (Gen. 1:1).	Cretaceous/Tertiary K-T extinction	Abundance of chalk	184 MY
			Dinosaurs on land, mosasaur in seas, and other mammals	Abundance of coal	
				Black shale (gas, oil, and other fossil fuel)	
	Jurassic		Major dinosaur species, first birds		
	Triassic		First dinosaurs	Ferns and gymnosperm, cycads, and conifers	
			Permian–Triassic extinction; all trilobites disappeared	Abundance of sand	
Paleozoic	Permian			Abundance of phosphate	300 MY
	Pennsylvanian		First reptiles	Floating forest formed abundance of coal	
	Mississippian		Sharks and amphibians were abundant	Ferns appeared	
	Devonian			Black shale (gas, oil, and other fossil fuel)	
	Silurian		First amphibians	Terrestrial plants	
	Ordovician				
	Cambrian		Shellfish	Explosion of complex animals suddenly appeared; twenty of thirty-six phyla existed	
			Clams		
			Trilobites		
			Jellyfish		
Precambrian	Formation of the earth		Banded iron formation; abundance of single-celled bacteria		4 BY

During the Precambrian era, it took almost four billion years for the earth to form. These bottom rocks are known as granite and basalt and were formed during this era.

A huge quantity of banded iron formation is in these Precambrian rocks, with 99.9 percent of iron mined from these rocks.

During the Cambrian period of the Paleozoic era, approximately 550 million years ago, complex creatures suddenly appeared. This is called the *Cambrian explosion*.

God created complex creatures, such as trilobites and other sea creatures. These Cambrian marine invertebrates appeared suddenly without any precursor in the preceding strata.

As previously mentioned, the animal kingdom is divided into thirty-six phyla. Twenty-seven of the thirty-six phyla can be found in fossil records, and twenty of the twenty-seven phyla appeared in the Cambrian explosion.

All things were made by Him, and without Him was not anything made that was made. (John 1:3)

Fish, terrestrial plants, first amphibians, sharks, and reptiles were created during the Paleozoic era, and minerals, such as iron and lead, formed during other periods of Paleozoic era.

First amphibians and terrestrial plants appeared during the Ordovician and Silurian periods of the Paleozoic era. Coal was produced abundantly during the Pennsylvanian period of Paleozoic era.

During the Permian period of the Paleozoic era, phosphate was produced in abundance. An abundance of sand was produced during the Permian–Triassic extinction event. Thick sand was deposited in North Africa, the Middle East, and throughout the world. The same sand was found in North America, Europe, and Asia. The Sahara Desert was formed by blowing the tops of these sand dunes.

The Sphinx is carved in these rocks, and the Treasury in Petra is known for its red sandstone walls.

The Paleozoic era, known as old life, ended abruptly and was called the Permian–Triassic extinction. All marine animals—which were plentiful, including complex creatures like trilobites—became extinct during this event.

Trilobites Graveyard

• During the extinction event, the animals were transported for long distances and buried by the sediments.

The new era, which is called Mesozoic (middle life), began approximately 250 million years ago. It has three periods known as Triassic, Jurassic, and Cretaceous. During the Mesozoic era, big and powerful dinosaurs roamed the earth, along with reptiles and mammals.

During the Triassic period, God created new sets of fauna and flora. Ferns and gymnosperms, like cycads and conifers, appeared and spread throughout the landscape. The first dinosaurs, which were small in size, started grazing through the landscape.

During the Jurassic period, major dinosaur species, like the long-necked dinosaurs called apatosaurus and stegosaurus, appeared, along with the first flying birds; the crow-sized archaeopteryx and pterosaurs dominated the skies. The Upper Jurassic period consisted of thick vegetation, and evergreen trees covered the earth. Sixty-feet tall ferns existed during this period.

During the Cretaceous period, life was abundant, and many species of animals and birds flourished. Tyrannosaurus rex, known colloquially as T-Rex, created havoc in the animal kingdom. Duck-billed dinosaurs, raptors, and dromaeosaurus roamed the land.

Dinosaurs

Velociraptor
(Velociraptor mongoliensis)

Pterosaur
(Pterosauria)

Stegosaurus
(Stegosaurus stenops)

Spinosaurus
(Spinosaurus aegyptiacus)

Brachiosaurus
(Brachiosaurus altithorax)

Allosaurus
(Allosaurus fragilis)

Plesiosaurus
(Plesiosaurus dolichodeirus)

Dilophosaurus
(Dilophosaurus wetherilli)

Archaeopteryx
(Archaeopteryx lithographica)

Parasaurolophus
(Parasaurolophus walkeri)

Triceratops
(Triceratops horridus)

Tyrannosaurus Rex
(Tyrannosaurus Rex)

Apatosaurus
(Apatosaurus ajax)

Mosasaurs ruled the seas, and sharks and crocodiles existed during the Mesozoic era. Life was good for all species on the land and in the seas. During the Devonian and the Cretaceous periods, black shale, from which gas, oil, and other fossil fuels are produced, was found in abundance. Most black shale is found in marine sediments and contains an abundance of organic matter. The modern-day fracking system was developed to extract gas and oil from the black shale.

Gymnosperm flora, consisting of conifers—evergreen trees, such as pine and spruce—cycads, and ginkgo existed during the Mesozoic era, as is evident from the fossil record.

The Mesozoic era began approximately 250 million years ago and is known as the age of reptiles and conifers. Dinosaurs, monstrous beasts, and mammals roamed the earth, and gymnosperm flora flourished during this era. Then one day, sixty-six million years ago, a devastating asteroid hit the earth with a great blow, and all animals and plants became extinct. The asteroid catastrophe preceded a prehistoric flood known as Zuni mega sequence recorded in the earth strata that brought landslides and mudslides, burying all living and nonliving things and ending the first creation.

Scientific evidence shows that an asteroid crashed to the earth at the Yucatan Peninsula with high velocity. The size of the asteroid was said to be six miles wide, and the earth was impacted beyond recognition.

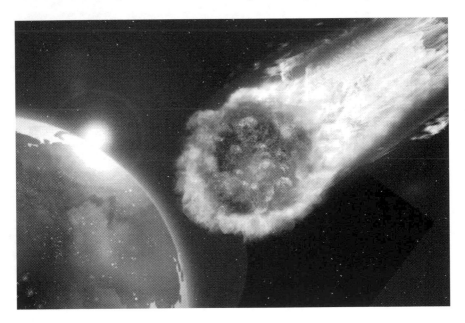

When the asteroid struck the earth during the Cretaceous period of the Mesozoic era, the following chain of events was triggered, which destroyed the earth and decimated life completely.

The asteroid was six miles wide and struck the earth at 40,000 miles per hour. It weighed trillions of tons.

The energy released was unimaginable and destroyed everything in its path, killing dinosaurs immediately; the animals in its proximity were vaporized.

The impact created tidal waves and earthquakes.

Immediately after the collision, billions of tons of debris and rocks that were thrown into skies later came down as fireballs, creating forest fires all over globe, killing everything away from the impact zone. This event is evident in United States, we can witness the ash or soot that spreads over an area that covered five states, also in other parts of the globe.

The continental drift

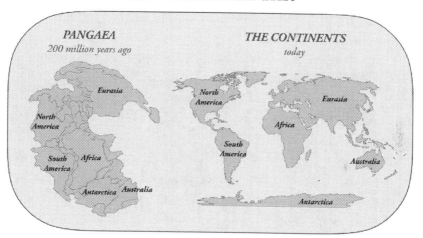

Mega-earthquakes, triggered by the asteroid catastrophe, broke off 50,000 miles of continental edges at the Pangea configuration, causing continental drift. At the same time, the subduction of ocean plates under the continental plates caused numerous earthquakes simultaneously raising Rocky mountain range in north American continent, Andes mountain range at south American continent and other mountains were raised throughout the globe. The subcontinent of India broke off from Pangea and moved north with high speed, crashing against the South Asia region and raising Mount Everest about 29,029 feet.

Due to the crash of the subcontinent of India to Asia, numerous volcanic eruptions took place, creating the Deccan Traps in western India. The Yellowstone volcano erupted during this time, as is evident by the sediment found around it. Mega-earthquakes triggered mega-tsunamis that were 1000 feet high and swept the globe, burying dead and living animals. It transported the dead carcasses for thousands of miles and dumped them in heaps. The global flood was very violent.

The rocks at the Lance and Hell Creek Formations contain thousands of dinosaur bones that were transported for long distances during Zuni mega sequence and dumped on continents with marine animals. The flood caused erosion in the earth's sediments, creating canyons and waterfalls throughout the world.

Rocks found on all continents are in the same sequence from bottom to top. You may not find the entire lithostratigraphic column at any given point, but whatever is found is in the same order, indicating all continents were together at the time of the asteroid catastrophe. Even similar fossils are found across the continents in the same order.

When the mega-earthquakes exploded all over the globe, they caused twelve to twenty feet of deformation in the rock layers. The heat produced by the change in direction of electromagnetic fields to abnormal levels caused rocks to melt and reset in their place. These rock folds can be seen in the Zagreb Mountains, the Grand Canyon, and Canada.

A few dinosaurs and birds were buried quickly and were fossilized with skin and whole body parts intact. Many of these animals' necks are arched back, indicating that the animals were trapped in the sediment and struggling to escape from the flood.

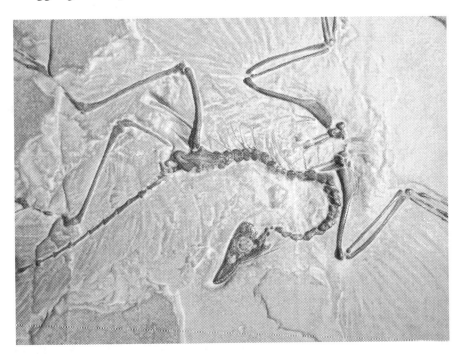

The asteroid strike caused a great impact in the sky, and the powers of the universe were shaken. The light- and energy-producing objects lost their power. The skies were no longer lit with the glory and wonders of the universe. The sun and stars were no longer able to dominate the skies. Darkness was everywhere for sixty-six million years, until the re-creation. The blackout that took place could not be understood or imagined. The sun and the stars remained in the skies as lifeless objects. The heavens that declare the glory of God and the firmament that showed his handiwork became obsolete. The magnificent glory, once radiant and visual, could not be seen for many years.

The earth was dormant for many millions of years, according to Genesis 1:2, just digesting the shock, pain, and tremors. During this period, for almost sixty-six million years, there was no life found in the earth's strata.

Twelve or thirteen dinosaurs fossils were found in a death pose, with the neck arched back, as if gasping for air. All dinosaurs became extinct during the asteroid catastrophe at the end of Cretaceous period. No dinosaur fossils have been found above the KT boundary, which is a strong indication that the asteroid impact on earth preceded a global flood that decimated life.

The earth was approximately 4.6 billion years old. Plants and animals existed for many years in the first creation, and the asteroid brought death and destruction to all the living creatures, including plants, sixty-six million years ago, prior to Genesis 1:2. There is geological evidence that shows the end of the Mesozoic era and the beginning of the present Cenozoic era, which is called the KT boundary, also known as the Cretaceous and Tertiary boundary.

It is the thin gray line, one inch to three inches in size, seen in all continents, and it contains clay and minerals, such as like iridium. Iridium is a very rare element found in the earth's crust, and high concentrations in this layer show that the asteroid crashed to the earth and brought epic devastation. The Precambrian, Paleozoic, and Mesozoic eras came to an end due to this destruction.

A fossil record is the record of dead animals that once lived during the first creation, especially the Paleozoic and Mesozoic eras, according to Genesis 1:1. Life in waters and on land were very diverse and plentiful. Fifty-seven classes and 230 orders of animals are extinct in the fossil record. At least 250,000 species have been identified in the fossil record that do not live in the present. Thorns, carnivory, disease, suffering, and death are evident in the fossil record.

The present world has been built with a tremendous and efficient decomposition system so that environment will not be affected due to the piling of dead carcasses. When an animal dies, the following occurs:

1. Scavengers eat the fleshy part of the carcass,
2. The skeleton is decomposed by bacteria and critters that live in the ecosystem.
3. The oxidation process reduces the rest to the earth.

The criteria for becoming a fossil are as follows: (1) <u>sudden burial</u>: flood dumps sediments on living animals; and (2) <u>constant supply of water and mineralization</u>: flesh and skeleton are replaced by minerals in the water (e.g., calcite, iron, and silica) so it becomes rock; eventually, rock preserves the animals. All the fossils found in the earth strata is due to the five mega sequences recorded in the earth history, they are known as Sauk, Tippecanoe, Kaskaskia, Absaroka and Zuni.

The fossil record shows the following:

- 95 percent consists of shallow marine organisms, like corals and shellfish, that lived during the Paleozoic and Mesozoic eras for almost 484 million years.
- 4 percent consists of algae, plants, and insects.
- 1 percent consists of all fish, amphibians, reptiles, birds, mammals, and dinosaurs that lived in Paleozoic and Mesozoic eras.
- Nearly 1.5 billion fossils have been found and preserved throughout the world.
- 200,000 trilobite fossils have been extracted from sediment throughout the world.
- 80 million fossil specimens exist in the British Natural History Museum.
- 1,000 well-preserved bat fossils can be seen in museums.

The Morrison Formation in Colorado has Jurassic-period dinosaurs remains caused by the fourth mega sequence known as Absaroka mega sequence, and the Lance Formation in Wyoming and South Dakota has tens of thousands of late-Cretaceous dinosaurs remains caused by the fifth mega sequence known as Zuni mega sequence. Apart from dinosaurs, the Lance Formation contains freshwater animals, like frogs and salamanders and marine fossils.

Approximately thirty nearly completed fossil examples of tyrannosaurs rex have been found. It was estimated that 2.5 billion T-Rex lived in the past.

The dinosaurs and marine fossils are found together on the land dumped by flood during Cretaceous–Tertiary extinction event.

Gymnosperm flora—conifers, cycads, and ginkgo—existed at Mesozoic era, as is evident in the fossil record.

The earth suffered a catastrophic event due to an asteroid. The beautiful earth that once enjoyed perfect balance underwent pain, with death everywhere. The life-producing tiny creatures lost their way. The living creatures on the land and in the seas became dead carcasses, with no one to bury them. All the living organisms, small and big, were gone. Sudden death came to this earth without warning.

The main casualties on the earth are said to be the dinosaurs. The beautiful and magnificent creatures that once roamed the earth and enjoyed life with power and strength were gone. Young and old had no hope of survival; it was a sudden extinction. The life in deep oceans that once thrived with lush vegetation and hot-water reefs vanished. The fish and other sea creatures suffered and faced dire consequences when death had seemed nowhere close. The asteroid catastrophe triggered a global flood, buried living things, and covered the whole earth.

TWO

THE SILENT YEARS OF THE EARTH AND THE SUN: THE BEGINNING OF THE TERTIARY PERIOD, CENOZOIC ERA

And the earth was without form and void and the darkness was upon the face of the deep. And the Spirit of God moved upon the face of the waters.

—Genesis 1:2

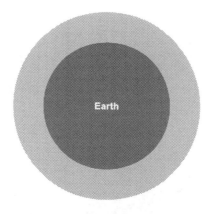

1. Empty without life.
2. Water covered the earth.
3. It was dark, and the Spirit of God hovered over the earth.

Genesis 1:2 is the beginning of the Tertiary period of Cenozoic era. It lasted almost sixty-six million years, until the re-creation in six days, seven thousand years ago in the Holocene epoch of the Quaternary period.

At this stage of the earth's history, no life was found in the earth strata. All living creatures, including bacteria and all types of flora, had been decimated. The Tertiary period includes the Paleocene, Eocene, Oligocene, Miocene, and Pliocene epochs; the Quaternary period includes the Pleistocene and Holocene epochs. These were completely submerged under universal ocean, according to Genesis 1:2, until the re-creation in Upper Holocene epoch.

The asteroid catastrophe preceded a prehistoric global flood, which brought landslides and mudslides, burying all living and nonliving things on earth. The huge earthquakes caused mega-tsunamis that destroyed the whole world. The air temperature increased to its highest levels, killing all land animals, and volcanos spilled lava and created an ecosystem disaster.

The myth of evolution that was being taught in the schools and universities ended abruptly. The tower of evolution came tumbling down with Genesis 1:2 because all life-forms were decimated, as is evident in the Tertiary rock layers for sixty-six million years. It gave rise to the re-creation, seven thousand years ago.

During Genesis 1:2, the following events occurred:

Geological features that are attributed to a global flood continued under a universal ocean that covered the whole earth for sixty-six million years, according to Genesis 1:2.

Erosion, or the shaving of the sediments, produced the Grand Canyon.

The top rocks are from the Permian period of the Paleozoic era. Apart from a few sediments here and there from the Triassic period, all other top sediments from the Jurassic and Cretaceous rocks were shaved off from the Grand Canyon. It is 277 miles long, eighteen miles wide, and a mile deep into the crust of the earth. The erosion by flowing waters carved one of the wonders of nature. Each layer tells the story of the earth. The rocks found at the bottom of the canyon are 1.8 billion years old.

The creation of waterfalls on many continents was also by erosion. Niagara Falls is a spectacular wonder in nature. Every second, 757,000 gallons of water flow over both falls combined, at American and Bridal Veil Falls at Niagara.

The scablands of Washington State were formed during same time as the Grand Canyon and Niagara Falls, due to erosion that took place under the global flood. The process continued under the universal ocean, according to Genesis 1:2. The name *scablands* was given because these lands were not suitable for farming. Dry Falls in the scablands and carved canyons were formed due to the prehistoric flood. Towers also were formed during global flood, followed by a universal ocean, according to Genesis 1:2.

Devils Tower in Wyoming.

Caves and pillars were carved by the global flood and continued under the universal ocean, according to Genesis 1:2. Mammoth Cave in Kentucky, Jewel Cave in Custer, South Dakota, and other caves in United States and on other continents were carved by the flood.

All the vertical walls of a canyon, gorge, caves, and arches are straight, solid rock. No loose material is seen, according to Genesis 1:2. After its formation, water covered the whole globe and removed the loose material. This happened for at least sixty to sixty-five million years.

The Cretaceous seafloor that accumulated for seventy-nine million years was eroded during the asteroid catastrophe. The present configuration of seafloors is from the Jurassic period sediments.

The rocks at the Lance and Hell Creek Formations in Wyoming and North Dakota, respectively, contain thousands of dinosaur bones that were transported for long distances and dumped on continents with marine creatures.

During this prehistoric global flood, the direction of the water current was consistently from east to west, as is evident in the geological records.

All the sediments, until the re-creation, includes the top Cretaceous and Tertiary layers are laminated, meaning there is no life found in the earth's strata. We can see the fossils of critters and organisms in the sediments, but they were not alive to mix up the soil (known as bioturbation). Every living organism was decimated, creating a formless and void earth, according to Genesis 1:2, which paved the way for God to rearrange the earth with humans during the re-creation, starting from Genesis 1:3. This is the reason Genesis 1:2 is detrimental to the evolution theory.

The condition of the earth—being covered with freshwater but not saltwater—remained for sixty-six million years, and it was the beginning of the Tertiary period of the Cenozoic era. The salt from oceans was destroyed and removed by the prehistoric flood and started to accumulate in the Tertiary period, sixty-two million years ago.

Carbon-14 (C14) presence in diamonds and in coal is because the earth was covered with water, according to Genesis 1:2, that acted like a trap in the sink so that no gases escaped into the atmosphere. Helium gas, which is one of the lighter gases trapped in the rocks, was due to the same fact—that the water covered the earth for sixty-six million years. The current rate of flow shows that it started to escape to the atmosphere seven thousand years ago, which proves that it took place after the re-creation.

The early scientific belief was that the earth was never covered with water, but the concept of plate tectonics shows that the earth indeed was covered with water and that continental drift took place under the universal ocean.

During this time, mega-earthquakes created violent situations with mega-tsunamis, and so much energy was released during the continental drift. During the asteroid catastrophe, the mega-earthquakes broke the edges of the present continents at fault lines from Pangea and moved to its present location during the period of Genesis 1:2; that is, for sixty-six million years. Continents were settling down in its new configuration, and mountains were raised and settling down.

Plate tectonics raised mountains on all continents. The subcontinent of India broke off from Pangea and moved north with high speed, crashing against the South Asia region, and raised Mount Everest to about 29,029 feet. At the same time, due to the crash of the subcontinent of India into Asia, numerous volcanic eruptions took place, creating the Deccan Traps in western India.

Mega-earthquakes took place, causing six to twenty or more feet of deformation in the sediment. Thousands of feet of sedimentary rocks were folded without any fractures due to excessive heat. The 1964 Alaskan earthquake, which was 9.2 on the Richter scale, caused eleven inches of deformation in the sediment. Folded rock layers in the Grand Canyon, the Zagreb Mountains of Turkey, and in Victoria, British Columbia, Canada happened during Genesis 1:2.

At one time, these mountain sediments were under the sea. During mountain building, continental plates collided against each other, raising mountains; thus, clams, fish, and other sea animal fossils have been found on top of the mountains.

Caves, arches, and pillars were formed during the entire duration of Genesis 1:2 for about sixty-six million years.

The present coal seams on the earth are similar in their formation and are found across the continents. They run from the eastern part of the USA to Europe and to the western part of Russia, indicating that all these continents were together during the Pangea configuration. Even the sediments and fossils that were found across the continents are similar, indicating these continents were together at one point.

The effects of the flood remained for sixty-six million years, and it was exactly as written in Genesis 1:2:

> And the earth was without form, and void; and darkness was upon the face of the deep. And the Spirit of God moved upon the face of the waters.

The condition of the earth, covered with water, remained for sixty-six million years; it was freshwater, not saltwater.

The earth was dormant for many years, digesting the shock, pain, and tremors, while there was blackness in the sky for the same duration.

In summary, the earth suffered a catastrophic event due to an asteroid. The beautiful earth that once enjoyed perfect balance underwent pain, with death everywhere. The life-producing tiny creatures lost their way. The living creatures on the land and in the seas became carcasses with no one to bury them. All the living organisms, small and big, were gone. Sudden death came to this earth without warning.

The main casualty on the earth has been said to be the dinosaurs. The beautiful and magnificent creatures that once roamed the earth with power and strength were gone. Young and old had no hope of survival; it was a sudden extinction. Life in the oceans, which once thrived with lush vegetation and reefs, vanished. Fish and other sea creatures suffered and faced dire consequences. The asteroid catastrophe that triggered the global flood known as Zuni mega sequence according to the scientific evidence buried the rest of the living things, covered the whole earth, and stood thousands of feet high above the surface, according to Genesis 1:2.

I believe that during the asteroid catastrophe, the extra water that appeared on the face of the earth during Genesis 1:2 came from the melting of the ozone layer that was present at the first creation. The composition of the ozone layer is O_3, which means three parts oxygen molecules. The asteroid entered the earth's atmosphere with high velocity, which caused great friction and heat that separated the O_3, and the hydrogen from outer space joined to create water molecules (H_2O) that came down as torrential rain and covered the earth.

THREE

THE RE-CREATION, DAYS ONE AND TWO, DURING THE QUATERNARY PERIOD, CENOZOIC ERA

What was the reason for the re-creation? Why did God create a second time when his creation was in an obsolete state? God values his creation, and he has a purpose. God created the beautiful universe once and filled the earth with life.

The answer lies in Isaiah 45:18:

> "For thus," saith the Lord that created the heavens, God Himself that formed the earth and made it. He hath established it. He created it not in vain, and He formed it to be inhabited, "I am the Lord; and there is no one else."

This is the heart of God. He values every creature he created with wisdom and knowledge. This very reason gave rise to God's re-creating the earth seven thousand years ago, when the earth was lifeless, and the Spirit of God was grieving and moaning for the loss of his creation by moving on the face of the waters.

During the six days of the re-creation, on which day was solid earth created?

The answer is that God did not create the solid earth a second time. There is not a second or third earth; one earth existed from the beginning with the original creation, according to Genesis 1:1, for 4.6 billion years.

> And I saw a new heaven and a new earth, for the first heaven and the first earth were passed away; and there was no more sea. (Revelation 21:1)

I want to bring your attention to one of the biggest discoveries in the creation account. Notice that the earth existed before day one of the re-creation, according to Genesis 1:3.

If solid earth existed under the water, then the solar system would have been in operational mode. We know that without the solar system, the earth cannot stay on its axis and go around the sun in its orbit. That means that both the sun and the earth existed before day one, but the condition of the sun was dark, with no light in it, according to Genesis 1:2.

What were the existing geological features of the earth at the time of re-creation? All seven continents were broken off from the Pangea configuration and settled in the new positions as North and South America, Europe, Asia, Australia, Africa, and Antarctica.

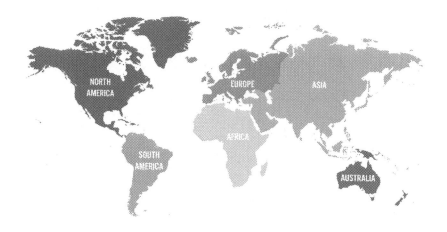

The mountains on all continents were raised and settled in place, as you see today.

A single universal ocean covered the entire globe, including all the continents and mountains. It appears that even though water covered the entire globe, there was no marine life. The water that covered the globe was freshwater, not saltwater. The salt from the oceans disappeared during the global flood. We can infer from the present salt found in the oceans that it started to accumulate sixty-two million years ago. An asteroid struck the earth sixty-six million years ago, and the earth experienced a violent situation until it settled down with a universal ocean.

DAY ONE OF THE RE-CREATION

> And God said, "Let there be light" and there was light. And God saw the light, that it was good, and God divided the light from the darkness. And God called the light day, and the darkness He called night. And there was evening and there was morning, one Day. (Genesis 1:3–5 ASV)

God started the re-creation seven thousand years ago. He brought forth the light (soft light) when he said, "Let there be light." The purpose of this light was to divide the day, which had a cycle of twenty-four hours of darkness. According to the Hebrew Bible, the literal translation of

Genesis 1:3, "Let there be light," is "Light be"; in other words, "Turn the light back on." The soft light that ruled the day during the first creation, as a backup light to the sun, was destroyed during the asteroid catastrophe. Thus, the night-and-day cycle began on day one, and it was twenty-four hours. (The earth's twenty-four-hour cycle existed from the first creation, according to Genesis 1:1.)

The Romans made the present twenty-four-hour day-and-night cycle division, which is right, according to the biblical explanation. According to Genesis 1:3, God divided the darkness by inserting twelve hours of daylight. For this reason, the day begins at 12:00:01 a.m. It has six-hour nights, plus twelve-hour day and six-hour night that ends at midnight (12:00:00). This pattern exactly matches at the equator and differs when it moves up or down toward the poles.

The main reason that God brought the light back was because the earth was rotating on its axis and going around the sun in the darkness for sixty-six million years; that is the entire duration of Genesis 1:2. The soft light that ruled the day during first creation as a backup light to sunlight that was destroyed during the asteroid catastrophe. Now, God brought the soft light back on day one of the re-creation to give light prior to reigniting the sun on the fourth day.

Let's talk about the twelve hours of soft light. This soft light is different from the sun's light. There is no piercing power in it, and it has no energy, in comparison with sunlight. You can notice it during dawn, dusk, and when the sky is covered with black clouds. This soft light is a backup light for the sun when the sun does not appear in the sky, when it rains or snows.

This soft light can move and spread everywhere, but sunlight moves straight and cannot be bent. Shadows are clearly visible in the sunlight but not so much with the soft light.

You can notice the soft light entering your home through glass windows and doors from all directions during dawn, dusk, and during cloudy days. This light is different from sunlight. Early in the morning before sun rises, soft light will enter the house from north, south, east and the west directions whereas sun light enters from east in the morning and from west in the evening.

When Grandma looks out the window and says it's a gloomy day, soft light is ruling the day.

With this creation of light, God separated the darkness, and he called it day.

> And God saw the light, that it was good, and God divided
> the light from the darkness. And God called the light day,
> and the darkness He called night. And there was evening
> and there was morning, one Day. (Genesis 1:4–5 ASV)

The Hebrew word for *day* is *yom*. Yom is used many times in the Bible with different meanings, such as day, forever, long time, and a season. Yom is always twenty-four hours in respect to the sun, moon and earth. There are twenty-four hours in a yom, and 365 yoms in a year.

<u>What is the significance of Bible mentioning one day, why not first day?</u>

> And God called the light day, and the darkness he called
> Night, And there was evening and there was morning, one
> day. (Genesis 1:5 ASV)

The scripture does not mention the first day; rather, the Hebrew words used here is *one day*. Here, the cardinal number, which in Hebrew is *yowmehad*, has been used for one day. Then the syntax changes to ordinal numbers to count the other days. The ordinal numbers are first, second, third, fourth, fifth, sixth, and seventh. Then the question arises: why wasn't the ordinal number used for one day? Why does scripture say *one day*? The Hebrew word *yowmehad* refers to a cardinal number—one day.

One, two, three, four, five, six, and seven are cardinal numbers. First, second, third, fourth, fifth, sixth, and seventh are ordinal numbers.

A child celebrates his or her *first* birthday because that child never had a birthday prior to that first birthday. It would be preposterous to call it his or her *one* birthday; that does not give any meaning. A couple celebrates their first anniversary because that couple didn't have an anniversary prior to that first anniversary.

The reason Bible says "one day" (not *first day*) is because the earth had days prior to one day. During the Precambrian, Paleozoic, and Mesozoic eras of the first creation, according to Genesis 1:1, the earth experienced the day-and-night cycle for many billions of years. The Cenozoic era began during Genesis 1:2. There was no daylight, but the earth was rotating twenty-four hours on its axis and moving in its orbit around the sun, 365 days a year, in the darkness until the re-creation. Genesis 1:1–2 covered 4.6 billion years.

Days Calculation Prior to One Day

4.6 billion years x 365 days/year
<u>4,600,000,000 x 365 days/year</u>
23,000,000,000
276,000,000,000
1,380,000,000

1,679,000,000,000

One trillion, 679 billion days existed prior to day one of recreation.

SECOND DAY OF THE RE-CREATION, SEVEN THOUSAND YEARS AGO

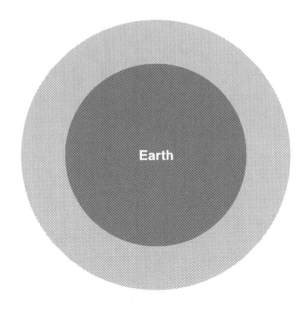

And God said, Let there be a firmament in the midst of
the waters, and let it divide the waters from the waters.
And God made the firmament and divided the waters
which were under the firmament from the waters which
were above the firmament, and it was so. And God called
the firmament heaven. And the evening and the morning
were the second day. (Genesis 1:6–8)

In Genesis 1:6, God divided the waters that covered the earth into two
parts. The outer water layer was pushed outward, creating a space called
sky/firmament (white color) between the inner and outer water layer as
shown in the diagram below. If this outer layer had stayed in liquid form,
that would have created an ecosystem disaster, and life would not have
been possible on the earth. For this reason, God turned this outer layer of
water into the ozone layer.

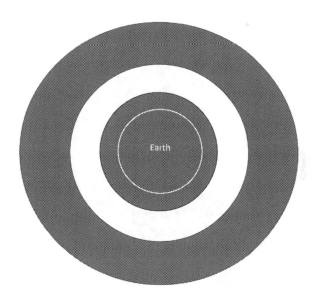

The outer water layer became the ozone layer when hydrogen
evaporated due to heat and friction, leaving a single molecule of oxygen.
This single oxygen molecule (O) combined with atmospheric oxygen (O_2),
forming the ozone layer (O_3). It is situated twenty to thirty miles above the

surface of the earth. Its main function is to protect all life-forms on earth by filtering two harmful forms of ultraviolet light called UV-B and UV-C.

This was the biggest hydraulic-lift operation that God performed on the second day.

Remember that the old ozone layer that was protecting the earth during the first creation was destroyed during the catastrophic asteroid event.

Apart from the ozone layer, the earth's magnetic field diverts the solar radiation wind away from the earth, which can be seen as the northern lights (aurora borealis) in the Northern Hemisphere and the southern lights (aurora australis) in the Southern Hemisphere.

The water, which was under the sky (between sky and earth)—that is, the inner water layer—later became the seas (Genesis 1:9). Thus, evening and morning were the second day.

Note: If the outer layer had remained in a liquid form, as a water canopy, it would not have allowed the sun's rays to enter the earth, which would have created an ecosystem disaster, and life would have been decimated on the face of the earth.

ISOSTATIC EQUILIBRIUM, OR ISOSTACY

The shifting of the rock beneath the earth's crust in response to the shifting in the weight above the earth's crust is known as *isostatic equilibrium*. On the second day, when the weight of the outer water layer was lifted, and on third day, when the weight of the inner water layer was lifted up from the whole earth, the continents and the mountains are experiencing the isostacy through upward and downward movement and adjusting to new positions.

The Appalachian Mountains are said to be three hundred million years old, and the Rocky Mountains are sixty-six million years old. Both mountain ranges are isostatically rebounding today and are experiencing small earthquakes continuously; this is because the weight of the universal ocean was eliminated seven thousand years ago. They are moving up and down to settle in their new positions, as indicated by their new height every year.

Significance of Firmament, or Sky

1. It is the place where clouds form through condensation, and precipitation takes place.
2. It contains atmospheric pressure that maintains the weather patterns.
3. It contains 78 percent nitrogen, 21 percent oxygen, and 1 percent other gases (e.g., argon, carbon dioxide) to maintain life on earth.
4. It is the place where birds and airplanes fly.

FOUR

DAYS THREE, FOUR, AND FIVE OF THE RE-CREATION

THIRD DAY OF THE RE-CREATION

> And God said, "Let the waters under the heaven be gathered together unto one place, and let the dryland appear," and it was so. And God Called the dry land earth; and the gathering together of the waters called He Seas; and God saw it was good. (Genesis 1:9–10)

On the third day, 29 percent of dry land appeared when the inner water layer receded to the seas according to Tejas known as the sixth mega sequence. Unlike the first five mega sequences in which the flood waters transgressed from Ocean to continents but during Tejas, the flood water was transgressing from continents to the seas or oceans throughout the globe. We have geological evidence in north America that the flood waters shaved off the Cenozoic sediments from the continent 7000 years ago and dumped it in the gulf of Mexico. When this process was completed, the continents we know now as North and South America, Europe, Africa, Asia, Australia, and Antarctica appeared.

And God called the dryland earth and the gathering together of the waters He called seas as shown in the diagram below, and God saw that it was good.

The Pacific, Atlantic, Antarctic, and Indian Oceans took their present form on the third day.

The first time the Atlantic Ocean was formed, a fault line was at the center of the ocean, running from north to south.

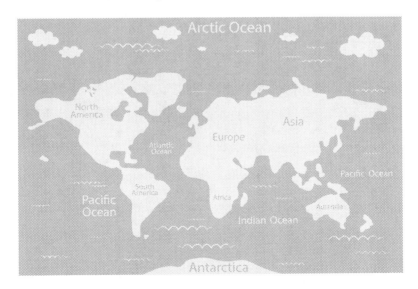

And God said, "Let the earth bring forth grass, the herb yielding seed, and the fruit tree yielding fruit after his kind, whose seed is in itself, upon the earth," and it was so. And the earth brought forth grass and herb yielding seed after his kind, and the tree yielding fruit, whose seed was in itself, after his kind; and God saw that it was good. And the evening and the morning were the third day. (Genesis 1:11–13)

The growth of vegetation took place not only at the location that God was creating but, on all continents, wherever the dry land appeared. The vegetation and trees had free rein to grow for 1,800 years before humans entered the continents after the Tower of Babel event.

On the third day, three types of vegetation showed up on all continents, according to its ecosystem:

1. Grasses
2. Herb-yielding seeds: herbal plants (e.g., basil, cilantro, dill, sage) grew in abundance. Seed grain plants: wheat, oats, barley, rice, and corn. Angiosperm flora, which is known as flowering plants, grew on all continents.

3. Fruit-bearing and other trees: apple, orange, mango, etc.; cypress; pine; spruce.

Note: The Bible is evidence-based because after asteroid strike, the earth was formless and void without any sign of life. It was completely covered with water for sixty-six million years. According to scientific evidence, grasses showed up for the first time in the fossil record during third day of the re-creation, seven thousand years ago in the Holocene epoch of the Quaternary period of the Cenozoic era. Prior to that, no life was found in the Tertiary and Quaternary periods for sixty-six million years.

"Methuselah," a bristlecone pine tree, thought to be the oldest living tree on earth, is about five thousand years old. It's located in the Inyo National Forest in California, and it appeared in the re-creation.

A coral reef in Australia is said to be 4,300 years old. The oldest hot-water reef known as Stromatolites from the first creation disappeared when the asteroid crashed into the earth.

FOURTH DAY OF THE RE-CREATION

> And God said, "Let there be lights in the firmament of the heaven to divide the day from the night and let them be for signs and for seasons and for days and years. And let them be for lights in the firmament of the heaven to give

light upon the earth," and it was so. And God made two great lights: the greater light to rule the day and the lesser light to rule the night. He made the stars also. And God set them in the firmament of the heaven to give light upon the earth, And to rule over the day and over the night and to divide the light from the darkness, and God saw that it was good. And the evening and the morning were the fourth day. (Genesis 1:14–19)

During the fourth day of re-creation, the sun, moon, and stars were not created new; rather, the Lord God ignited the sun and the stars with fire and with the right amount of power and energy to give light because there was a blackout for sixty-six million years, according to Genesis 1:2.

God made two great lights. The Hebrew word used here is asah, which is translated in English as "made." Asah means "to work with" or "to be made."

When the earth was covered with darkness, there was absence of light from the sun known as "The faint young sun paradox" according to the scientific evidence. For this reason, God had to light/fine-tuned the sun to sustain the vegetation, which he created on the third day.

The sun is the main energy source for the earth. God created the photosynthesis process for vegetation to survive. Sunlight gives vitamin D to animals and humans, who were created on the fifth and sixth days.

And God said, "Let there be lights in the firmament of the heaven to divide the day from the night and let them be for signs and for seasons and for days and years." (Genesis 1:14)

During the re-creation of the earth, on fourth day, God made two greater lights to give light on earth; it was for signs and for seasons and for days and years.

Let's talk about seasons. A season was a new concept during the re-creation of the earth after the asteroid catastrophe. The earth runs its course of seasons—summer, fall, winter, and spring—due to a 23.5-degree tilt as it goes around the sun in its ecliptic orbit.

During the Precambrian, Paleozoic, and Mesozoic eras, however, the earth's tilt was missing. The earth rotated on its true north and south axes in an orbital/elliptical plane around the sun. For this reason, the earth's weather condition was tropical at the ecliptic plain and cooler at the poles without ice caps. Under the ice caps, we can see evidence of lush vegetation that once thrived during the first creation. At the equator, due to high temperatures, reefs were abundant and were produced in the hot water by bacteria known as Stromatolites. They were found at the latitude of 40 degrees north and south from the equator, compared to the present reef made up of coral at 15 degrees north and south latitude from the equator. The ecosystem was completely different from the present ecosystem; snow and ice were absent during the first creation.

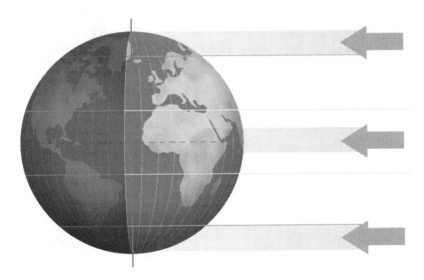

The animals that lived during the Paleozoic and Mesozoic eras were gigantic compared to the present era. The dinosaurs were huge, and the pterosaurs dominated the skies, with a forty-foot wingspan. The fossil record shows that it was more diverse—250,000 species that were found in the fossil record are absent from the present world, with few exceptions. All sorts of critters, trilobites, and ammonites dominated the ecosystem.

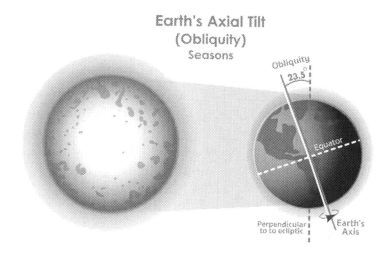

Earth's Axial Tilt
(Obliquity)
Seasons

When did earth get its 23.5-degree tilt? It was during Cretaceous and Tertiary mass extinction event, triggered by an asteroid. The asteroid, which was six miles wide, struck the earth at the Yucatan Peninsula in Mexico. The exact location, which was present at the Pangea configuration, is hard to locate since the continents moved to the new locations after the catastrophe.

The continental drift

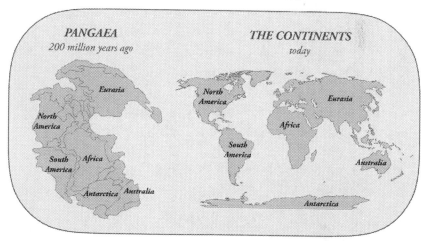

> And God set them in the firmament of the heaven to give
> light upon the earth. (Genesis 1:17)

Let's change the words *set them* to *fine-tuned them* for better understanding. The fine-tuning and the restoration of the sun took place on the fourth day, seven thousand years ago. God reignited the sun and the stars to their previous glory with the right power and energy to sustain life on the earth. There are numerous—tens and hundreds—of anthropic principles that are right to sustain life on the earth. Here are just four examples of anthropic principles:

1. The sun is ninety-three million miles away from the earth, which is an ideal distance to maintain life on earth. If the sun were a little bit closer, life, as we know it, would be impossible due to excessive heat. If the sun were a little bit farther away, life, as we know it, would be impossible due to excessive cold.
2. The rotation of the earth—1,060 miles per hour—is perfectly designed. If the earth's rotation was slightly faster, it would not hold things on the surface but would throw things into space, and life would not exist. If the earth's rotation was a little bit slower, the earth would freeze during night and burn during daytime.
3. The sun is in the center of our solar system, and all planets rotate perfectly around the sun. Mercury and Venus are placed between the sun and the earth to absorb the excessive radiation produced by the sun. Mars, Jupiter, Saturn, Uranus, and Neptune are placed on the other side of the earth to protect it from comets and space rocks from the outer space.
4. The ozone layer and electromagnetic field regulate and allow just the required radiation to sustain life on earth.

Many more anthropic principles exist that boggle the mind when we think of our great Creator.

> And to rule over the day and over the night and to divide
> the light from the darkness, and God saw that it was good.
> (Genesis 1:18)

Characteristics of Soft Light

Dawn (ruled by soft light) 6:00–7:00 a.m.		During rain and snow, soft light rules the dawn.
Daylight (ruled by sun) 7:00 a.m.–5:00 p.m. (sunrise to sunset)		During rain and snow, soft light rules the day.
Dusk (ruled by soft light) 5:00–6:00 p.m.		During rain and snow, soft light rules the dusk.

The sun is the main energy source for the earth, but another functions of the sun is to divide the light from darkness.

The soft light that was created on day one is very noticeable on cloudy days and when it rains or snows. It is not noticeable on sunny days, as sunlight is more powerful than soft light.

FIFTH DAY OF THE RE-CREATION

And God said, "Let the waters bring forth abundantly the moving creature that hath life and fowl that may fly above the earth in the open firmament of heaven." And God created great whales and every living creature that moveth, which the waters brought forth abundantly, after their kind, and every winged fowl after his kind, and God saw that it was good. And God blessed them, saying, "Be fruitful and multiply and fill the waters in the seas, and let fowl multiply in the earth." And the evening and the morning were the fifth day. (Genesis 1:20–23)

These sea creatures sprang up in the oceans, seas, and rivers, according to the weather conditions and ecosystems. Some of the sea creatures were the same as in the first creation, and some were newly created.

SEA ANIMALS

| Whale | Octopus | Dolphin | Turtle |

| Shark | Killer whale | Narwhal |

| Sperm whale | Beluga whale | Squid |

| Sea Horse | Angler | Blowfish | Jellyfish |

The blue whale, which was created during the re-creation, is bigger in size compared to dinosaurs. The sharks reappeared in the re-creation and dominated the ocean and the seas.

The birds were created on all continents, according to the natural weather patterns. God knows what is best for his creation. Eleven thousand species of birds exist today.

The firmament, which was created on the second day of creation, is mentioned in Genesis 1:20: "And fowl that may fly above the earth in the open firmament of heaven."

The space created by God by moving the outer water layer above the earth created the space for birds to fly, and eventually, the waters became the ozone layer.

God blessed them and said they should be fruitful and multiply. These two characters, "fruitful and multiply," dominated his creation.

Some of the sea creatures lived in the first creation and the re-creation. Clams, paddlefish, lobster, squid, jellyfish, stingrays, turtles, and sharks have been found in the fossil record.

FIVE

THE RE-CREATION, DAY SIX

FIRST PART OF THE SIXTH DAY OF THE RE-CREATION

And God said, "Let the earth bring forth the living creature after his kind, cattle and creeping thing and beast of the earth after his kind," and it was so. And God made the beast of the earth after his kind and cattle after their kind and everything that creepeth upon the earth after his kind, and God saw that it was good. And God said, "Let us make man in Our image, after Our likeness and let them have dominion over the fish of the sea and over the fowl of the air and over the cattle and over all the earth and over every creeping thing that creepeth upon the earth." So, God created man in His own image, in the image of God created He him, male and female created He them. And God blessed them, and God said unto them, "Be fruitful and multiply and replenish the earth and subdue it and have dominion over the fish of the sea and over the fowl of the air and over every living thing that moveth upon the earth." (Genesis 1:24–28)

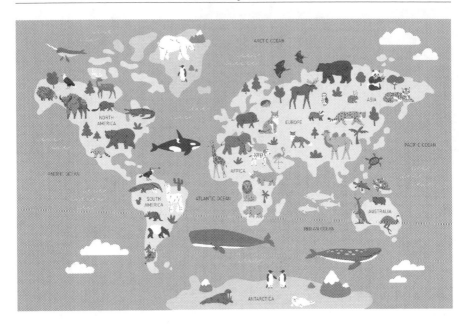

So, on the sixth day, God brought different kinds of animals on the land. And God said to replenish the earth because the first creation was destroyed during the asteroid catastrophe.

Notice that the dinosaurs were missing in the re-creation due to their dominance and aggressiveness.

At the command of the Lord God Almighty, the earth brought forth the animals, each according to its kind. This event did not take place in a particular location but throughout the earth on all continents, simultaneously and spontaneously, wherever there was dry land. On the third day, 29 percent of dry land appeared when the inner water layer receded to the seas.

Three thousand species of mammals were created during the sixth day. They were created male and female to adapt to the weather conditions and ecosystems on land and to grow and multiply. Different kinds of apes, monkeys, gorillas, predators (such as big cats), and prowling predators and mammals appeared on the face of the earth. Polar bears, snow leopards, and penguins appeared at the poles; kangaroos in Australia; llamas and anteaters in South America; large bison in North America; big cats, like cheetahs and lions in Africa; and camels appeared in Asia and Africa.

Three types of animals were brought forth,

1. Herbivore (mammals, including domesticated animals)
2. Carnivore (beasts of the field, like lion and tigers)
3. Omnivore (bears, chimpanzees, badgers)

These animals multiplied on all continents, twenty, thirty, forty, and even fifty centuries before humans placed their feet on these continents. Humans started moving out from the Mesopotamia region after the event of the Tower of Babel and found that vegetation and animals existed in those regions.

Humans never evolved from animals, as evolution suggests.

Hominids are the family of apes, such as gorillas, orangutans, and chimpanzees, who lived in the wooded areas and did not evolve to humans. These animals were brought forth by God on the sixth day.

> Then God said, "Let the earth bring forth the living creatures." (Genesis 1:24)

All present animals showed up on all continents wherever dry land existed on the sixth day. All animals that you see today and many animals that were extinct in the absence of humans for many centuries showed up instantly. Three thousand species of mammals appeared on all continents.

The ape family showed up on all continents, according to their kind. According to fossil records, they dominated in Spain, South Africa, and China because that's where the oldest bones of these animals were found. These were not human bones. The male-to-female ratio was almost 50 percent. Their average age was thirty-five years, according to fossil records. When teeth were examined under the microscope, it was found these animals were omnivorous.

Gorillas, chimpanzees, Australopithecus afarensis (Lucy), Australopithecus africanus, Homo erectus, and Homo neanderthalensis belong to the bipedal ape family. God never breathed the breath of life into any animal, not in the first creation or during re-creation, Seven thousand years ago. They are special creatures in the sight of God, created for humans to have dominion over them and to take care of his creation.

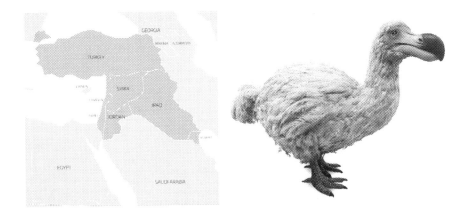

God told Adam to spread across the world to have dominion over the fish of the sea, over the birds of the air, and over every living thing that moved on the earth (Genesis 1:28).

When humans disobeyed God's command and stuck to the Mesopotamia region, many species became extinct in the absence of man for twenty, thirty, forty, and even fifty centuries on many continents. Some of the extinct animals and birds are the wooly mammoth, saber-toothed tiger, wooly rhinoceros, and the dodo bird etc.

The animals and birds that escaped extinction during the ice age and earthquakes multiplied on all continents before the humans arrived. Humans started spreading out from the Mesopotamia region after the Tower of Babel event, and they found animals and vegetation existed in those regions.

Insects and reptiles lived in both the first creation and the re-creation. These include the following found in the fossil record:

Insects—spider, beetle, lizard, centipede, crickets, cockroach, stinkbug, centipedes, termite, dragonfly, and scorpion

Reptiles—snake, turtle, lizard, and crocodile

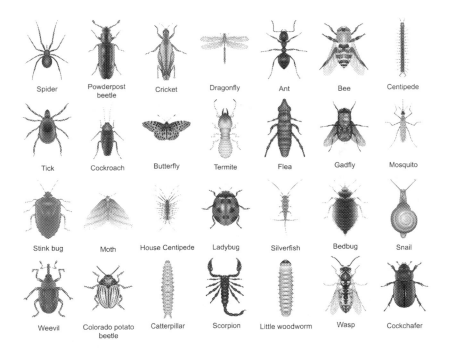

Spider	Powderpost beetle	Cricket	Dragonfly	Ant	Bee	Centipede
Tick	Cockroach	Butterfly	Termite	Flea	Gadfly	Mosquito
Stink bug	Moth	House Centipede	Ladybug	Silverfish	Bedbug	Snail
Weevil	Colorado potato beetle	Catterpillar	Scorpion	Little woodworm	Wasp	Cockchafer

SECOND PART OF THE SIXTH DAY OF THE RE-CREATION

And God said, "Let us make man in Our image, after Our likeness and let them have dominion over the fish of the sea and over the fowl of the air and over the cattle and over all the earth and over every creeping thing that creepeth upon the earth." So, God created man in His own image, in the image of God created He him, male and female created He them. And God blessed them, and God said unto them, "Be fruitful and multiply and replenish the earth and subdue it and have dominion over the fish of the sea and over the fowl of the air and over every living thing that moveth upon the earth." (Genesis 1:26–28)

Genesis 1:26–28 gives us a summary of God's creating Adam and Eve on the second part of the sixth day and commissioning them to rule over the creatures that he created on the fifth and sixth day. The details, however, are written in the next chapter. Genesis 2:7–25 is the explanation of how Adam and Eve were created.

The explanation in Genesis 2 is not a new creation account; rather, it is the continuation of the sixth day. It might surprise many because the description is in chapter 2, but it does not fall into contention because there are no chapter divisions in the original Hebrew Bible.

SECOND PART OF THE SIXTH DAY OF THE RE-CREATION IN GENESIS 2

Creation of Adam and Eve

And the Lord God formed man of the dust of the ground, and breathed into his nostrils the breath of life; and man became a living soul. The Lord God planted a garden eastward in Eden, and there He put the man whom He had formed. And out of the ground the Lord God made every tree grow that is pleasant to the sight, and good for food. The tree of life also in the midst of the garden, and the tree of knowledge of good and evil.

And a river went out of Eden to water the garden, and from thence it was parted, and became into four heads. The name of the first is Pishon; that is, it which compasseth the whole land of Havilah, where there is gold. And the gold of that land is good; there is Bdellium and the onyx stone. And the name of the second river is Gihon: the same is it that compasseth the whole land of Ethiopia. And the name of the third river is Hiddekel: that is it which goeth toward the east of Assyria. And the fourth river is Euphrates.

And the LORD God took the man, and put him into the garden of Eden to dress it and to keep it. And the LORD God commanded the man, saying, Of every tree of the garden thou mayest freely eat: But of the tree of the knowledge of good and evil, thou shalt not eat of it: for in the day that thou eatest thereof thou shalt surely die."

And the LORD God said, It is not good that the man should be alone; I will make him an help meet for him." And out of the ground the LORD God formed every beast of the field, and every fowl of the air; and brought them unto Adam to see what he would call them: and whatsoever Adam called every living creature, that was the name thereof. And Adam gave names to all cattle, and to the fowl of the air, and to every beast of the field; but for Adam there was not found an help meet for him.

And the LORD God caused a deep sleep to fall upon Adam, and he slept: and he took one of his ribs, and closed up the flesh instead thereof; And the rib, which the LORD God had taken from man, made he a woman, and brought her unto the man. And Adam said, This is now bone of my bones, and flesh of my flesh: she shall be called Woman, because she was taken out of Man." Therefore shall a man leave his father and his mother, and shall cleave unto his wife: and they shall be one flesh. And they were both naked, the man and his wife, and were not ashamed. (Genesis 2:7–25)

Genesis 1:26–31 is the summary of events that took place in the second half of the sixth day. God made animals in the morning of the sixth day and said, "It is good." The detailed description of the creation account of Adam and Eve is not found in Genesis 1 but in Genesis 2:7–25. It should not be considered a new and different account, in comparison with Genesis 1; rather, it is the continued description of events that happened on the second half of the sixth day.

Let us explore in detail:

> And the LORD God formed man *of* the dust of the ground and breathed into his nostrils the breath of life; and man became a living being. (Genesis 2:7)

God formed Adam from the dust of the ground, indicating that Adam was made (asah) from the existing material.

God breathed into his nostrils the breath of life, and the man became a living being. This act of God was unique because God never breathed the breath of life into sea creatures, birds of the air, or land-dwelling animals when they were brought forth into existence. For this reason, Adam was unique—he was made from existing material at the same time that he was created with the breath of life from God and became a new creature, one that never had existed during any eras of earth history.

Humans are different from animals because we have bodies, souls, and spirits, and animals have only bodies and souls.

> The LORD God planted a garden eastward in Eden, and there He put the man whom He had formed. (Genesis 2:8)

Adam was created outside the garden, and later, God placed him in the garden of Eden, which was the special place where God and humans met to have a fellowship in the cool of the day.

> And out of the ground the LORD God made every tree grow that is pleasant to the sight and good for food. The tree of life *was* also in the midst of the garden, and the tree of the knowledge of good and evil. (Genesis 2:9)

These trees were made (asah) especially in the garden of Eden, which were different from the trees that appeared throughout the continent on the third day of the re-creation. Four types of trees showed up in the garden. They were as follows:

1. Pleasant to the eyes
2. Good for food
3. Tree of life
4. Tree of the knowledge of good and evil

These trees were made especially for Adam to enjoy his days in the garden.

> And a river went out of Eden to water the garden, and from thence it was parted, and became into four heads. (Genesis 2:10)
>
> The name of the first *is* Pison; that is *it* which compasseth the whole land of Havilah, where *there is* gold. (Genesis 2:11)
>
> And the gold of that land *is* good. There is Bdellium and the onyx stone. (Genesis 2:12)
>
> And the name of the second river *is* Gihon; the same *is* it that compasseth the whole land of Ethiopia. (Genesis 2:13)
>
> And the name of the third river *is* Hiddekel; that is, it which goeth toward the east of Assyria. And The fourth river *is* the Euphrates. (Genesis 2:14)

God created four rivers, the starting point of which was the garden of Eden, indicating the garden was situated at a higher elevation so that water would flow downstream. At present, we don't have four rivers that have same starting point, but two of four rivers still exist in the Mesopotamia region: Tigris (Hiddekel) and Euphrates.

And the LORD God took the man, and put him into the garden of Eden to dress it and to keep it. (Genesis 2:15)

And the LORD God commanded the man, saying, "Of every tree of the garden thou mayest freely eat." (Genesis 2:16)

"But of the tree of the knowledge of good and evil, thou shalt not eat of it, for in the day that thou eatest thereof thou shalt surely die." (Genesis 2:17)

The main job that God appointed to Adam was to tend and keep the garden. He could eat from all trees, including from the tree of life, except from the tree of knowledge of good and evil.

And the LORD God said, "*It is* not good that the man should be alone; I will make him an help meet for him." (Genesis 2:18)

When Adam was bored with living alone in the garden of Eden, God decided to make a suitable helper or companion.

And Out of the ground the LORD God formed every beast of the field and every fowl of the air; and brought *them* unto Adam to see what he would call them. And whatsoever Adam called every living creature, that *was the name thereof.* (Genesis 2:19)

Note: In comparison to the morning creation on the sixth day, this creation of animals in the garden was different.

And Adam gave names to all cattle, and to the fowl of the air, and to every beast of the field; But for Adam there was not found an help meet for him. (Genesis 2:20)

God formed different animals and birds and asked Adam to name every animal that God formed out of the ground in the garden. These animals were domestic, and their kinds are associated with humans even today:

- Domesticated animals, like pets (dog, cat)
- Livestock (cattle, sheep, pig, goat)
- Beast of the field (horse, camel, donkey)
- Birds of the air (chicken, turkey)

Adam named them all, but none of these animals was found suitable to be his helper because they were different from him.

> And the LORD God caused a deep sleep to fall upon Adam, and he slept; and He took one of his ribs, and closed up the flesh instead thereof. (Genesis 2:21)

> And the rib, which the LORD God had taken from man, made He a woman, and brought her unto the man. (Genesis 2:22)

> And Adam said, This *is* now bone of my bones And flesh of my flesh; She shall be called Woman, Because she was taken out of Man. (Genesis 2:23)

> Therefore shall a man leave his father and his mother, and shall cleave unto his wife, and they shall be one flesh. (Genesis 2:24)

> And they were both naked, the man and his wife, and were not ashamed. (Genesis 2:25)

When God created Eve, he blessed them and said, "Be fruitful and multiply." These two characters God placed in all his creation; even the stars were multiplying and spreading in the space. Animals and plants have the capacity to reproduce and multiply in abundance.

Since we are created in the image of God, we can do and achieve greater things that animals cannot achieve.

And God said, "Behold, I have given you every herb *bearing* seed, which *is* upon the face of all the earth, and every tree, in the which is the fruit of a tree yielding seed; to you it shall be for meat." (Genesis 1:29)

And to every beast of the earth, and to every fowl of the air, and to everything that creepeth upon the earth, where in *there is* life, *I have given* every green herb for meet; and it was so." (Genesis 1:30)

THE SIGNIFICANCE OF GOD GIVING VEGETARIAN DIET TO ADAM AND EVE AND THE CATTLE

And God said, Behold, I have given you every herb bearing seed, which is upon the face of all the earth, and every tree, in the which is the fruit of a tree yielding seed; to you it shall be for meat. (Genesis 1:29–30)

The question arises here: why did God tell Adam and Eve to eat vegetables and fruits, not meat?

In the early days of Adam and Eve, the knowledge and use of a knife was unknown, and the concept and use of fire was not yet perfected. There was no Costco or BJ's, where Eve could run and buy a dressing knife, and they did not know how to use fire. They had to discover the use of a knife and fire later in their lives. If God had told them to eat meat, they would have eaten raw meat, like wild animals, and gotten sick, and that would have been the end of the human race on the face of the earth. God knew this problem and protected Adam and Eve by giving them the vegetarian diet.

In Genesis 9:3, God gave permission to Noah and his family to eat meat. One might ask, why now? Why it was wrong to eat meat in Genesis 1 but OK to eat meat in Genesis 9?

The answer is found in Genesis 8:20–21:

And Noah builded an altar unto the Lord; and took of every clean beast, and of every clean fowl, and offered burnt offerings on the altar. And the LORD smelled a sweet savour; and the LORD said in His heart, "I will not again curse the ground any more for man's sake; for the imagination of man's heart *is* evil from his youth; neither will I again smite any more everything living, as I have done."

When Noah offered the burnt sacrifice, God saw that the use of fire had been perfected by humans. In the very next chapter, after six verses, God gave them permission to eat meat. Now they could barbecue the meat and enjoy their meal.

And God saw everything that He had made, and, behold, *it was* very good. And the evening and the morning were the sixth day. (Genesis 1:31)

THE SIGNIFICANCE OF "EVENING" AND "MORNING" DURING THE RE-CREATION

The account of evening and morning is mentioned in the scriptures at the end of each day, except for seventh day because God stopped his creation work on the seventh day and rested.

The significance of scriptures mentioning evening and morning was not anything other than what Adam and Eve experienced that day. Adam and Eve were created in the second half of the sixth day. Adam was first created outside the garden, sometime in the late morning, and God prepared a special place called the garden of Eden and brought him there to live.

God created domestic animals to accompany him and asked Adam to name these animals. When God did not find a suitable partner for Adam, he created Eve out of Adam's rib and brought her to Adam as a suitable companion around evening.

Now, as brand-new humans, for the first time they saw and experienced the sunset—dusk preceded the night on sixth day; then sunrise—dawn preceded daylight on the seventh day. (For this reason, even today, Jews celebrate the sabbath beginning at sunset on Friday until the next sunset.)

Since Adam and Eve saw and experienced sunset, evening and morning have been associated with the biblical description of the day. This strongly indicates that the creation account of Genesis was passed on to subsequent generations by Adam.

- Adam lived 243 years with Methuselah.
- Methuselah lived ninety-eight years with Shem. Now Shem has information about the creation account, as well as the flood account.
- Shem lived fifty years with Isaac, Abraham's son.
- Isaac lived forty-five years with his grandson Levi, Jacob's son.
- Levi lived with Amram for unknown years in Egypt. (The years count was lost in Egypt.)
- Amram, the father of Moses, lived with his son for many years when they left Egypt. During Moses's stay with his people in Egypt and later on their journey in the wilderness, Moses gathered the Genesis account from the slaves for the first time.

How can we be certain that the creation account that Moses wrote in Genesis 1 is true?

We can trust the creation account wholeheartedly because the Word of God is absolute and infallible.

Secondly, Moses spent forty days and nights in the presence of God Almighty at Mount Sinai, where he had a chance to clarify the Genesis account with the Creator himself, who was the only eyewitness when he created the heaven and the earth in the beginning. And Moses received the tablets with the Ten Commandments, which were written by the finger of God Almighty on the mountain of God.

SIX

FIRST CREATION AND THE RE-CREATION

FOSSIL RECORD OF FIRST CREATION AND THE RE-CREATION

Sixty-six million years sets apart the fossil records of the first creation and re-creation, from the KT extinction event that took place at the end of the Mesozoic era to the re-creation that took place seven thousand years ago. Therefore, numerous differences have been identified in the fossil record. They are as follows:

1. All the fossils from the Paleozoic and Mesozoic eras are found below the KT boundary.
2. No trilobite, dinosaur, Pteranodon, or mosasaurus fossils were found above the KT boundary, which is called the Cenozoic era.
3. 250,000 species that lived during the first creation are absent from the re-creation.
4. Dinosaur and human fossils never coexist in the fossil record, due to the gap of sixty-six million years between them.
5. Three thousand mammal species are living today; none of these fossils is found below the KT boundary but are in Quaternary sediments, less than seven thousand years ago.

6. Eleven thousand species of bird that live today were never found during the first creation, with few exceptions. Bats and other birds lived in both creations.

7. The whales, dolphins, and other sea creatures appeared during the re-creation seven thousand years ago for the first time; they were absent in the first creation. Sharks and coelacanth fish, however, lived in the first creation and re-creation.

8. 250,000 species of angiosperm, known as flowering plants, never existed during the first creation. Very few flowering plants that existed during the Upper Cretaceous period are found below the KT boundary.

9. Some of the sea creatures lived in both the first creation and re-creation: clams, paddlefish, lobster, squid, jellyfish, shells, stingray, coelacanth, turtle and shark are found in the fossil record.

10. Insects lived in both the first creation and re-creation:_spider, beetle, lizard, crickets, cockroach, stinkbug, centipedes, termite, dragonfly and scorpion are found in the fossil record.

11. Reptiles lived in both the first creation and re-creation: snake, turtle, lizard, and crocodile are found in the fossil record.

God knew the benefit of these creatures in their respective ecosystems and brought them forth in both the first creation and the re-creation.

BIBLICAL SUPPORT FOR FIRST CREATION AND THE RE-CREATION: BARA AND ASAH

Numerous scripture evidence is found throughout the Bible for the first creation and the re-creation.

> Then God blessed the seventh day and sanctified it, because in it He rested from all His work which God had created and made. (Genesis 2:3)

The Hebrew words bara and asah are mentioned in verse three.

> These are the generations of the heavens and of the earth when they were created, in the day that the Lord God made the earth and the heavens. (Genesis 2:4)

The first creation and the re-creation have been explained clearly by these verses. Let's divide verse four into two parts. The first part says, "These are the generations of the heavens and the earth when they were created."

Genesis 1:1 states, "In the beginning God created the heaven and the earth." Many other translations say *heavens*. The Hebrew word used here for "created" is *bara*—bringing something out of nothing—and it is considered as a brand-new beginning.

The heaven and the earth created in the beginning is his first creation. This creation, according to scientific evidence, has three eras: Precambrian, Paleozoic, and Mesozoic. The heaven or universe was created 13.8 billion years ago and the earth 4.6 billion years ago.

Life on earth during the Paleozoic and Mesozoic eras was abundant with different species of sea creatures, land animals, and gymnosperm flora. The sky was dominated by forty-foot-winged pterosaurs, and dinosaurs roamed the earth for at least 186 million years. The fossil record is the record of the first creation, which was created according to Genesis 1:1.

The re-creation was explained clearly by the second part of Genesis 2:4, which says "in the day that the Lord God made the earth and the heavens." Notice here the word used is *made*; in Hebrew, it is asah. We all know the difference between create and make. Create means bringing something out of nothing, and asah means bringing out something from the existing material. Even the sequence mentioned here matches the re-creation.

Here, it says "in the day that the Lord God made the earth and heaven." Re-creation took place seven thousand years ago, according to Genesis 1:3. The earth was formed during first three days, and the sun and stars were reignited on the fourth day.

On day one, light was created to separate the day from night (soft light). According to the Hebrew Bible, the literal translation of Genesis 1:3 ("Let there be light") is "Light be"; in other words, "Turn the light back on." The soft light that ruled the day during first creation, as a backup light to sunlight, was destroyed during the asteroid catastrophe.

On second day, God made firmament. Again, the word used here is *made* because the earth already existed, according to Genesis 1:2, and the previous sky collapsed during the asteroid catastrophe at the end of the first creation. The waters that covered the earth, according to Genesis 1:2, was divided into two parts. The outer water layer was pushed outward to make the firmament once again, and this outer water layer became the ozone layer eventually.

On third day, the inner water layer was drained to the oceans and seas so that 29 percent of dry ground appeared, according to the present configurations. When dry land appeared, God brought grass and trees to grow on all continents, wherever there was dry land.

On fourth day, God made two great lights. Again, the word *made* (asah) is used for the sun and moon because they were already in existence. The Lord God had to reignite the sun and stars because they were not giving light. We know that the sun, moon, and stars that were created, according to Genesis 1:1, were in existence throughout Genesis 1:2 and continued to Genesis 1:3 during re-creation.

The earth would not have existed without the solar system, which upholds all the planets, so that it rotates on its axis and orbits around the sun. If the sun was created on day four, then the existence of earth, according to Genesis 1:2, and first three days of the re-creation were impossible. That is why Genesis 2:4 is a very important verse—it gives the summary of two creation-model accounts, according to Genesis 1.

According to Genesis 1:2, "that the earth *was* without form and void and the darkness was upon the face of the deep. And the Spirit of God moved upon the face of the waters."

The English translation of the verb *was* is *haytah* in the original Hebrew Bible, meaning "became." The brief explanation is that the earth, once beaming with life, *became* formless and void due to an asteroid catastrophe. In Genesis 1:2, we see the effects of the asteroid strike, which preceded a global flood; it decimated the first creation and left the earth formless and void. After the global flood, the world was radically different, and the recovery was long—almost sixty-six million years before the re-creation.

SECOND BIBLICAL SUPPORT FOR FIRST CREATION AND THE RE-CREATION

"Water stood above the mountains."

The second evidence for the re-creation is found in Psalm 104:6—"thou cover it with the deep as with a garment: the waters stood above mountains."

During the asteroid catastrophe, the prehistoric flood decimated the first creation and covered the whole earth, including all the high mountains that were present:

> The earth was without form and void; the darkness was upon the face of the deep and Spirit of God was moving upon the face of the waters. (Genesis 1:2)

At present, we don't have the same amount of water that was present during Genesis 1:2, covering all the high mountains, unless we reverse the process that took place on the second day during the re-creation. On the second day, God separated the waters into two parts. The outer water layer was pushed outward to make sky, which later became the ozone layer, and the inner water layer became the seas and oceans on the third day so that 29 percent of the dry land that exists appeared. According to my calculations 70 percent of water that was present during Genesis 1:2 was taken up in the outer water layer.

I believe that during the asteroid catastrophe, the extra water that appeared on the face of the earth during Genesis 1:2 came from the melting of the ozone layer that was present at the first creation. The composition of the ozone layer is O_3, which means three parts oxygen molecule. The asteroid entered the earth's atmosphere with high velocity, which caused great friction and heat that separated the O_3, and the hydrogen from outer space joined to create water molecules (H_2O) that came down as torrential rain and covered the high mountains.

The next verses give us the picture of the second-day event when God divided the waters into two parts. The outer water layer was pushed outward to make firmament, and the inner water layer was drained off from mountaintops and valleys to run to the oceans,(according to Tejas mega sequence) the place that God had set for them.

> Thou coveredst it with the deep as with a garment: the waters stood above the mountains. At thy rebuke they fled; at the voice of thy thunder, they hasted away. They go up by the mountains; they go down by the valleys unto the place which thou hast founded for them. (Psalm 104:6–8)

The second part of Psalm 104:9 says "that they turn not again to cover the earth."

Third Biblical Support for First Creation and the Re-Creation

"World then was perished."

The third evidence for the first creation and the re-creation is found in 2 Peter 3:4–7.

> And saying, Where is the promise of his coming? for since the fathers fell asleep, all things continue as they were from the beginning of the creation. For this they willingly are ignorant of, that by the word of God the heavens were of old, and the earth standing out of the water and in the water: Whereby the world that then was, being overflowed with water, perished: But the heavens and the earth, which are now, by the same word are kept in store, reserved unto fire against the day of judgment and perdition of ungodly men.

Second Peter 3:5 says in the second part that "by the word of God the heavens were of old, and the earth standing out of water and in the water." It clearly explains the first creation, which is very old, according to Genesis 1:1, and is considered to be 13.8 billion years for the heavens and 4.6 billion years for the earth.

Second Peter 3:6 says, "Whereby the world that then was, being overflowed with water, perished."

This does not indicate Noah's flood because the whole world did not perish for the three following reasons:

1. Noah and eight of his family survived.
2. The animals on the ark did not perish.
3. The animals that lived on the continents outside of the Mesopotamia region survived.

All dinosaurs and plant fossils found in the sediments are from the first creation, according to Genesis 1:1, which was decimated due to the asteroid catastrophe that preceded the prehistoric global flood that caused the beautiful earth to perish, according to Genesis 1:2. The present world in which we live was re-created in six days, seven thousand years ago. Adam and Eve were created during this present time, and their generation will face the judgement when Jesus comes again.

FOURTH BIBLICAL SUPPORT FOR FIRST CREATION AND THE RE-CREATION

The fourth evidence for the second creation is found in Exodus 20:11, which says,

> For in six days the Lord made heaven and the earth, the sea and all in them is, and rested the seventh day: wherefore the Lord blessed the sabbath day and hallowed it.

God emphasized the day of rest, known as the Sabbath for humans, without attempting to tell us that the whole creation was done in six days.

Here, Moses again emphasized the word *made* (asah in Hebrew). This is exactly what happened during the re-creation, according to Genesis 1:3. The earth was formed during the first three days, and the sun and stars were reignited on the fourth day. It was not a creation account, according to Genesis 1:1.

Fifth Biblical Support for First Creation and Re-Creation

Fall of Lucifer with one-third of angels

Theological explanations found in the Bible give rise to the theory of the earth's being without form and void, why darkness covered the earth, and the effects of an asteroid.

> How art thou fallen from heaven, O Lucifer, son of the morning! how art thou cut down to the ground, which didst weaken the nations! For thou hast said in thine heart, I will ascend into heaven, I will exalt my throne above the stars of God: I will sit also upon the mount of the congregation, in the sides of the north: I will ascend above the heights of the clouds; I will be like the most High. Yet thou shalt be brought down to hell, to the sides of the pit. (Isaiah 14:12–15)

This event indicates a huge turn during the first creation, when Lucifer, one of the archangels, rebelled against God. A battle took place in heaven, and Lucifer, with his minions, were thrown out of heaven. This story seems just a joke for many people, but it provides a significant correlation with scientific evidence.

Let's explore more on this topic. What did Jesus say?

> And he said unto them, I beheld Satan as lightning fall from heaven. (Luke 10:18)

Jesus is relating the fall of Satan to the past event, when he was thrown out of heaven with one-third of angelic forces. When Satan rebelled against God, he was thrown out of heaven and fell to the earth.

> The thief cometh not, but for to steal, and to kill, and to destroy: I am come that they might have life, and that they might have it more abundantly. (John 10:10)

The earth was decimated completely during the asteroid catastrophe, which can be attributed to the fall of Satan. The example to steal, kill, and destroy can be applied to the beautiful earth that once beaming with the diverse life of fauna and flora during the first creation.

This event—the fall of Satan—caused a great impact in the sky, and the powers of the universe were shaken. The light and energy-producing objects lost their power. The skies were no longer lit to see the glory and wonders of the universe. The sun and stars were no longer able to dominate the skies. Darkness was everywhere for sixty-six million years known as "The faint young sun paradox". The blackout that took place was not understood or imagined. The sun and the stars remained in the skies as lifeless objects. The heavens that declared the glory of God and the firmament that showed his handiwork became obsolete. The magnificent glory, once radiant and visual, was not seen for many years. At the same time, due to the instability in the sky, the asteroid hit the earth with a great explosion.

The earth suffered one of the great disasters in history, and the blow destroyed all ecosystems, including the ozone layer. A great explosion caused the magnetic field to rise to its highest levels. Fire rained from the skies and increased the temperature; the heat rose to such high levels that it caused the rocks to fold ninety degrees because they lost their hardness and became soft.

According to scientific evidence the whole solar system was hit hard during this time. It was bombarded with space rocks or meteorites.

Planet Venus: - One hundred percent of Venus' surface was overturned by the cosmic bombardments, and it changed the direction of its rotation. It is rotating clockwise which is opposite to the rotation of the earth.

Planet Mars: - Fifteen percent of the Mars surface is overturned by the cosmic bombardments.

Planet Uranus: - Due to cosmic bombardment, the planet Uranus got almost ninety-eight-degree tilt and it is rotating on its side. Also, it rotates clockwise which is opposite to the rotation of the earth.

Moon: - The other side of the moon which is not visible to the earth has scars that cover fifteen percent of the surface.

SIXTH BIBLICAL SUPPORT FOR FIRST CREATION AND RE-CREATION

> For the creature was made subject to vanity, not willingly, but by reason of him who hath subjected the same in hope, Because the creature itself also shall be delivered from the bondage of corruption into the glorious liberty of the children of God. For we know that the whole creation groaneth and travaileth in pain together until now. And not only they, but ourselves also, which have the firstfruits of the Spirit, even we ourselves groan within ourselves, waiting for the adoption, to wit, the redemption of our body. For we are saved by hope: but hope that is seen is not hope: for what a man seeth, why doth he yet hope for? But if we hope for that we see not, then do we with patience wait for it. (Romans 8:20–25)

According to the above scripture, whole creation groans along with the children of God and waits for deliverance and redemption. The application of the cause is twofold:

1. The first creation was destroyed against its will.
2. There was the fall of Adam and the effects of sin upon the creation and on the children of God.

The first creation was destroyed against its will. Life on earth during the Paleozoic and Mesozoic eras was abundant with different species, both on the land and in the sky. One day, without any warning, the asteroid struck the earth, and followed by a global flood that decimated all life on the face of the earth and left it *Tohu Va bahu*—the English translation is "without form and void," which is equivalent to futility.

The destruction during first creation was not due to God's judgment; rather, it was the work of the enemy. God allowed the destruction to take place against its will in the same way as he gave permission to test Job in the Old Testament. God had a plan to re-create and bring humans on the earth to have fellowship with him and to conquer sin and death by sending his Son to die for us and redeem us. When the earth was lying lifeless, the Spirit of God was grieving and moaning for the loss of his creation by moving on the face of the waters. The Spirit of God saw the fossils of the dead animals in the earth's strata for sixty-six million years. If it was God's judgment, the Spirit of God would not have been moving upon the waters, as indicated by Genesis 1:2.

> And I saw a new heaven and a new earth, for the first heaven and the first earth were passed away, and there was no more sea. (Revelation 21:2)

The whole creation, including the universe, solar system, earth, and children of God will be redeemed completely with glorious liberty at Jesus's Second Coming.

In summary, the creation of heaven preceded the earth during first creation, and the earth preceded the sun during re-creation. Three eras existed in the first creation, and only one era continued, with Genesis 1:2 onward, into the re-creation (i.e., Genesis1:3). Continents were formed and stayed together during the first creation, and continental drift took place during the Cenozoic era, according to Genesis 1:2. Continents were in their present locations at the time of re-creation, seven thousand years ago.

Note: All scientific discoveries correlate with the two-creation model of first creation, 13.8 billion years for heaven and 4.6 billion years for the earth. Re-creation took place in six days, seven thousand years ago, according to Genesis 1:1–3.

SEVEN

EVOLUTION, THE SABBATH, AND RAIN

EVOLUTION IS A MYTH AND A LIE

The evidence for theistic creation has far greater truths than the theory of evolution because God existed before Genesis 1:1. God created the heaven and earth in the beginning. The concept of evolution is a pernicious theory, and it lacks evidence.

It is a myth and a lie because it goes contrary to the creation account. The dichotomy of creation and evolution poses uneasiness in the minds of people and brings conflict of worldviews.

During the Cambrian period of the Paleozoic era, approximately 550 million years ago, complex creatures suddenly appeared; this was called the Cambrian explosion. The Cambrian explosion poses a challenge to evolution. The sudden appearance of species in the Cambrian explosion was a great surprise for scientists because fully formed animals appeared in the fossil record.

God created complex creatures, like trilobites and other sea creatures. These Cambrian marine invertebrates appeared suddenly, without any precursor in the preceding strata.

The animal kingdom is divided into thirty-six phyla, and twenty-seven of the thirty-six phyla can be found in fossil record. Twenty out of thirty-six phyla appeared in the Cambrian explosion.

> All things were made by Him, and without Him was not anything made that was made. (John 1:3)

We can be 100 percent sure that evolution never happened; rather, God brought these animals into existence.

EVOLUTION'S TREE OF LIFE IS A DUD

The late Dr. Stephen J. Gould brought two great truths during his lifetime. He was a famous paleontologist, an evolutionist, and an atheist from Harvard University. He noticed that the animals suddenly appeared and stasis until they disappeared from the scene. This is the pattern we see in the actual fossil evidence.

In contrast to creation, the "tree of life" that was promoted by Charles Darwin has no evidence to prove that the single-celled bacteria evolved to complex animals; the fossil record does not support it. The simple-to-complex theory has no basis because these Cambrian marine invertebrates appeared suddenly, without any precursor in the preceding strata, and were complex creatures.

The word *trilobite* indicates that the complex animal was made with three lobes.

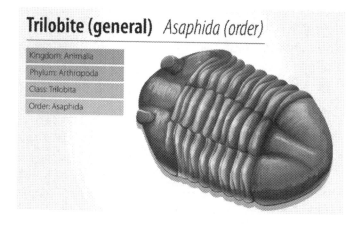

Trilobite (general) *Asaphida (order)*

Kingdom: Animalia
Phylum: Arthropoda
Class: Trilobita
Order: Asaphida

Unlike the composition of our eyes, a trilobite's eye was made without organic tissue but by calcite, as in limestone. Trilobites had compound eyes, consisting of several separate lenses (at least six) that gave 360-degree vision in the water.

NO TRANSITIONAL FORMS WERE FOUND

Charles Darwin stated, "If my theory be true, numberless intermediate varieties … most assuredly have existed." It is well-known that a missing link was never found in the earth's history.

As Darwin admitted in 1859,

> Geology assuredly does not reveal any such finely graduated organic chain, and this, perhaps, is the most obvious and serious objection which can be urged against the theory. The explanation lies, as I believe, in the extreme imperfection of geological records.

After 150 years of exhausting and strenuous research by numerous paleontologists and thousands of dollars spent, not a single significant transitional animal fossil was found.

Nearly 1.5 billion fossils have been found and preserved throughout the world, and 200,000 trilobite fossils have been extracted from the sediments throughout the world.

Thirty-two nearly complete T-Rex fossils have been found in the world.

Eighty million specimens exist in the British Natural History Museum from five major groups, but no transitional form was found in it.

One thousand well-preserved bat fossils can be seen in museums.

> In the beginning God created heaven and the earth. (Genesis 1:1)

> All things were made by Him, and without Him was not anything made that was made. (John 1:3)

The debate between science and faith is futile, and the debate between science and religion is a waste of time. Faith and true science should go hand in hand because the God who created the universe is the God of science.

Life on earth did not evolve; it was created. When God created the living beings, he designed the magnificent and complex cell to produce its own kind. This cell is like a factory and has 3.5 billion genetic codes hidden in it. It has the information to produce its own kind, and it cannot produce any other kind. Evolution never gives us absolute answers; rather, it only speculates. Life never originated by chance; it was God's creation.

It is time to reconsider whether evolution does justice to humankind if we do not dismantle it.

NO LIFE WAS FOUND IN GENESIS 1:2

> And the earth was without form, and void; and darkness was upon the face of the deep. And the Spirit of God moved upon the face of the waters. (Genesis 1:2)

At this stage of the earth's history, there was no life found in the earth's strata. All living creatures, including bacteria, and all types of flora were completely decimated.

The asteroid catastrophe preceded the prehistoric global flood that brought landslides and mudslides, burying all living and nonliving things on the face of the earth.

The huge earthquakes took place, causing mega-tsunamis that destroyed the whole world. The temperature increased to its highest level, killing all land animals, and volcanos spilled lava and created an ecosystem disaster. The environment was affected drastically.

You might think that since the water covered the earth, the marine creatures survived. The Bible says, however, that the earth was empty, without any life. For this reason, on the fifth day, God brought forth all sea creatures into existence.

The myth of evolution that's taught in the schools and universities ended abruptly. The tower of evolution came tumbling down with Genesis 1:2 because the animals in Darwin's tree of life and all life-forms were decimated, and this gave rise to the re-creation.

HUMANS DID NOT EVOLVE FROM ANIMALS

The re-creation began seven thousand years ago. On the sixth day, God brought forth all land animals, including hominids, which belong to the ape family, such as gorillas, orangutans, and chimpanzees, who lived in the wooded areas and did not evolve to humans.

> Then God said, "Let the earth bring forth the living creatures." (Genesis 1:24)

All present animals showed up, according to their kind, on all the continents wherever dry land existed; that is, 29 percent of land mass. All animals that you see today and many animals that were extinct in the absence of humans for many centuries showed up instantly. Three thousand species of mammals appeared on all continents on the sixth day, according to the weather patterns and ecosystem.

Fossil record show that these hominids dominated in Spain, South Africa, and China because that's where the oldest bones of these animals were found. These are not human bones. The male-to-and female ratio was almost 50 percent. and their average age was thirty-five years, according to the fossil record. When a tooth was examined under the microscope, it was found that these animals were omnivorous.

These hominids still exist today in wooded areas. They are bipedal but are not the ancestors of humans, as evolution allegedly suggests. They belong to the animal kingdom but not to human lineage. Adam and Eve were created and made in God's image, according to Genesis 5:1.

Humans are created in the image of God and can achieve greater things that no other animals can achieve. *Image of God* means that we have body, soul, mind, and spirit. That is why we can reason with many ideas, and those ideas can be transferred through the brain to the body to produce the result. It is like a technology written with the help of science. That technology was later transferred to AutoCAD and sent to a machine to produce a tool. The brain is the catalyst to observe the information. We can lead productive and meaningful lives because we are created in the likeness of God. Humans were created and made by God, not part of an evolution process.

EFFECTS OF DISOBEDIENCE BY EARLY HUMANS

God told Adam to spread across the world to have dominion over the fish of the sea, the birds of the air, and every living thing that moved on the earth (Genesis 1:28).

When humans disobeyed God's command and stuck to the Mesopotamia region, many species became extinct in the absence of man for twenty to fifty centuries on many continents. Animals like the saber-toothed tiger, wooly mammoth, and wooly rhinoceros and birds like the dodo bird and many others became extinct during re-creation.

If early humans had reached the continents, many animals probably would have been saved through nature's conservatory programs, like what we have today.

SABBATH DAY

> Thus the heavens and the earth were finished, and all
> the host of them. And on the seventh day God ended his
> work which he had made; and he rested on the seventh day
> from all his work which he had made. And God blessed
> the seventh day, and sanctified it: because that in it he had
> rested from all his work which God created and made.
> (Genesis 2:1–3)

The Sabbath day was ordained by God Almighty through the Ten Commandments. During the re-creation, in six days God made the earth, but on the seventh day, God rested from creating.

> He made known his ways unto Moses, his acts unto the
> children of Israel. (Psalm 103:7)

When Moses wrote the Pentateuch, especially the book of Genesis, there was no trace of a Sabbath followed or celebrated by anybody. Moses first wrote of the "Sabbath day" in Exodus 20:11.

There was no trace of a Sabbath celebrated by Adam or his children, Noah, or Abraham, and the children of Israel never kept the Sabbath until they ended up in Egypt as slaves. Every day, they worked. In Genesis 1, God made the earth and heaven in six days and rested on the seventh day.

God rested on the seventh day, not due to the exertion of creating first creation and re-creation in six days. God Almighty is omnipotent and will not get tired like us. When we think about the various aspects of creation that took place throughout the first creation, beginning from Genesis 1:1, and during re-creation, seven thousand years ago, humans were on God's mind. Humans were his crowning creation; that's why he sent his Son to die and redeem us from the curse and sin. God set a precedent for humans to follow—six days of work and one day of rest, which is ideal for the whole human race, everywhere on this globe.

The Sabbath is a special day because God stopped creating animals and birds after the sixth day. For this reason, new kinds of animals or birds don't appear in nature every day. Also, the Sabbath day is not to be considered as an infinite day on earth because there was an eighth day after the seventh day, and the day and night cycle will continue until Jesus comes again.

ORIGIN OF RAIN

The book of Genesis is called the book of origins because in it, we see the origin of the universe and the earth; the origin of life on earth, including plants, animals, and humans; the origin of disobedience and sin; the origin of family; the origin of murder, and the origin of government. Also, it gives us the origin of rain.

God brought back the rain and water system during the re-creation. For the duration of Genesis 1:2—almost sixty-six million years—the earth never saw the rain because of the universal ocean and the firmament (sky) did not exist at that time.

> And every plant of the field before it was in the earth, and every herb of the field before it grew: for the LORD God had not caused it to rain upon the earth, and there was not a man to till the ground. But there went up a mist from the earth, and watered the whole face of the ground. (Genesis 2:5–6)

The scientific word for a mist (mentioned in Genesis 2:6) is *evaporation.* That gives us a strong understanding of the water cycle that we see on the face of the earth.

There is evidence of rain, found in the fossil record, occurred during the first creation, especially during the Precambrian, Paleozoic, and Mesozoic eras. Raindrops were captured in a fossil record preserved in South Africa and is said to be 2.7 billion years old.

Genesis explains the origin of rain that was brought back before the creation of Adam and Eve. It happened on the sixth day, between the time that the animals were brought forth on all continents and the creation of Adam. The water cycle today has four components,

1. Evaporation
2. Condensation

3. Precipitation
4. Watering the earth, which runs back to oceans through creeks and rivers

Evaporation takes place when the ocean surface water is heated due to the sun's energy and becomes gas. It rises up to form clouds through condensation and precipitation, enabling it to drop back to earth in freshwater form to sustain life on earth.

> He who builds His layers in the sky, And has founded His strata in the earth; Who calls for the waters of the sea, And pours them out on the face of the earth. The LORD *is* His name. (Amos 9:6)

The Bible gives us the exact account of the water cycle. Condensation and precipitation allow the rain to water the whole earth, and it runs back to the oceans from wherever the water cycle began.

> All the rivers run into the sea, Yet the sea *is* not full; To the place from which the rivers come. (Ecclesiastes 1:7)

WHAT DID GOD DO DURING FIRST CREATION AND IN RE-CREATION?

In the beginning, God created heaven and the earth, which includes whole cosmos, sky, and solar system. Once the earth was formed, at an appropriate time, God started creating different creatures, plants, earth materials, and different metals during first creation, keeping humans on his mind. God knew exactly what was needed for humans to live, thrive, and have dominion over the earth. During the Cambrian period of the Paleozoic era, God created complex sea creatures like trilobites and, later, different types of marine vertebrates, amphibians, insects, and land animals.

During the Mesozoic era God created various species of dinosaurs and, later, birds like the forty-foot-winged pterosaurs. The ecosystems were unique compared to the present, and large hot water reefs existed during the first creation.

Paleozoic and Mesozoic rocks contain different earthly deposits, like shale, limestone, and sandstone; metals like iron, copper, lead, and aluminum; and precious metals, like platinum, diamond, gold, and silver. Black shale, from which gas, oil, and fossil fuels are extracted, helps humans every day to overcome energy requirements. The formation of coal during the Pennsylvania and Cretaceous periods was abundant and sustained humans by providing energy for many centuries. God was building ecosystems, a good environment, and the right atmosphere for humans to flourish on the earth.

During the Cenozoic era God rearranged the earth, grass, and trees on the third day, and he reignited the sun and stars on fourth day, sea creatures and birds on the fifth day, and land animals, insects, and humans on the sixth day. During this era, God created 250,000 species of flowering plants; 3,000 species of mammals; and 11,000 species of birds.

Adam and Eve were God's crowning creation because they were made in his own image. We are made a little lower than the angels (Hebrews 2:7). God created heaven and earth, keeping humans on his mind so that, one day, humans would know him and have fellowship with him.

Genesis 1 is literal when we use logical reasoning, scientific evidence found in the earth strata, and theological support from the Bible.

Also, the rock strata known as the lithostratigraphic column proves the different eras classified as Precambrian, Paleozoic, Mesozoic, and Cenozoic. The fossils in the rocks prove the magnificent creative power of God from the beginning of time. Heavens filled with galaxies with billions of stars, and our solar system—with other planets, earth, moon, and sun—declares the glory of God, day and night without fail.

The creation account from the Bible is literal, as it is the absolute, infallible, and inerrant Word of God.

Printed in the United States
by Baker & Taylor Publisher Services